ephesians

A DOUBLE-EDGED BIBLE STUDY

ephesians

A DOUBLE-EDGED BIBLE STUDY

NAVPRESS
Discipleship Inside Out™

TH1NK: **Life**Change™

NAVPRESS

Discipleship Inside Out™

NavPress is the publishing ministry of The Navigators, an international Christian organization and leader in personal spiritual development. NavPress is committed to helping people grow spiritually and enjoy lives of meaning and hope through personal and group resources that are biblically rooted, culturally relevant, and highly practical.

For a free catalog go to www.NavPress.com
or call 1.800.366.7788 in the United States or 1.800.839.4769 in Canada.

contents

introduction to TH1NK: LifeChange

Double-Edged and Ready for Action

For the word of God is living and active. Sharper than any double-edged sword, it penetrates even to dividing soul and spirit, joints and marrow; it judges the thoughts and attitudes of the heart.

Hebrews 4:12

a reason to study

Studying the Bible is more than homework. It is more than reading a textbook. And it is more than an opportunity for a social gathering. Like Hebrews suggests, the Bible knows us, challenges us, and, yes, judges us. Like a double-edged sword, it's sharp enough to cut through our layers of insecurity and pretense to change our lives forever.

Deep down, isn't that what we want – to actually *experience* God's power in our lives through Scripture? That's what TH1NK: LifeChange is all about. The purpose of this Bible study is to connect you intimately with God's Word. It can change you, not only intellectually but also spiritually, emotionally, maybe even physically. God's Word is that powerful.

The psalmist wrote,

> *What you say goes, GOD,*
> *and stays, as permanent as the heavens.*
> *Your truth never goes out of fashion;*
> *it's as up-to-date as the earth when the sun comes*
> *up. . . .*
> *If your revelation hadn't delighted me so,*
> *I would have given up when the hard times came.*
> *But I'll never forget the advice you gave me;*
> *you saved my life with those wise words.*
> *Save me! I'm all yours.*
> *I look high and low for your words of wisdom.*
> *The wicked lie in ambush to destroy me,*
> *but I'm only concerned with your plans for me.*
> *I see the limits to everything human,*
> *but the horizons can't contain your commands!*
>
> (PSALM 119:89-90,92-96, MSG)

Do you notice the intimate connection the psalmist has with God *because* of the greatness of the Word? He trusts God, he loves Him, and his greatest desire is to obey Him. But the only way he knows how to do any of this is because he knows God's voice, God's words.

the details

Each TH1NK: LifeChange study covers one book of the Bible so you can concentrate on its particular, essential details. Although every study covers a different book, there are common threads throughout the series. Each study will do the following:

1. Help you understand the book you're studying so well that it affects your daily thinking
2. Teach valuable Bible study skills you can use on your own to go even deeper into God's Word
3. Provide a contextual understanding of the book, offering historical background, word definitions, and explanatory notes
4. Allow you to understand the message of the book as a whole
5. Demonstrate how God's Word can transform you into a bona fide representative of Jesus

Every week, plan on spending about thirty to forty-five minutes on your own to complete the study. Then get together with your group. Depending on the amount of time it takes, you can either go through a whole or a half lesson each week. If you do one lesson per week, you'll finish the study in just under three months. But it's all up to you.

the structure

The twelve lessons include the following elements:

Study. First you'll study the book by yourself. This is where you'll answer questions, learn cultural and biographical information, and ask God some questions of your own.

Live. After you've absorbed the information, you'll want to look in a mirror – figuratively, that is. Think about your life in the context of what you've learned. This is a time to be honest with yourself and with God about who you are and how you are living.

Connect. You know that a small-group study time isn't just for hanging out and drinking soda. A small group provides accountability and support. It's one thing to say to yourself, *I'm really going to work on this* and entirely another thing to say it to a group of your friends. Your friends can support your decisions, encourage you to follow through, and pray for you regularly. And vice versa.

In your group, you'll want to talk with each other about what you discovered on your own, things that went unanswered, things that challenged you, and things that changed you. Use the guidance in this section to lead your discussion. After that, pray for each other.

Go deeper. Thirsty for more? Just can't get enough? Then use the guidance in this section to explore even deeper the vastness of Scripture. It's similar to extra credit for all you overachievers who love to learn.

Memory verse of the week. Did a particular verse make you think? Is there a verse you can't get out of your head? Write it down and memorize it. Allow God's Word to permanently brand itself in your head and your heart.

Notes from group discussion. At the end of each chapter, there are some pages for notes. Use them to ask questions of God or yourself, to write important verses and observations, or for anything else you want to jot down.

now go!

You are now ready to experience God and the Bible in an intense new way. So jump in headfirst. Allow the double-edged sword of Scripture to pierce your mind, your heart, your life.

Introduction to Ephesians

broadened horizons

It's easy, especially in this media-saturated culture, to feel like you can get the full story on just about anything. Want the whole truth? Well then, complete information is just an Internet search away. Knowledge – it's what's for dinner.

But the early churches didn't have Google; instead, these first Christians relied on letters of instruction and teaching from the church founders, apostles like Paul. And while many of the apostle Paul's letters found in the New Testament were written to address a specific error in spiritual thinking or activity, Ephesians was different. Instead of focusing on one particular heresy, Paul wrote Ephesians with the specific intent of broadening his readers' spiritual horizons to help them grasp the mission and purpose God had for them.

The truth of Ephesians is simple: God, through His grace, has given us each an eternal purpose. A mission to carry out. Paul's hope is that those who read it, including us, will have our horizons broadened further than even the reaches of the Internet.

setting: the urban outfitter

Ephesus was a major urban center in ancient Asia, a region that overflowed with prosperity. A port city, Ephesus was a center of trade between Asia Minor and Italy (and the biggest and best of Asia's seven urban centers), which led to its overwhelming cosmopolitan nature. It was full of wide streets, enormous public buildings, and luxurious homes, most of which were created to impress tourists. Ephesus also boasted a 25,000-seat theater and dozens of temples, the greatest of which was the Temple of Artemis, four times the size of the Parthenon and one of the Seven Wonders of the World.

As for society, Ephesus was ruled by a council made up of one hundred aristocrats who governed the city as a favor for the Roman Empire. These aristocrats also owned most of the surrounding land and the major industries, so they were, to say the least, fabulously wealthy.

Still, Ephesus thrived because of its large number of merchants, businessmen, and craftsmen, some of whom achieved wealth, but nothing like that of the ruling aristocrats. So the deal worked like this: The wealthy aristocrats ruled the city, and everyone else just did their jobs. Opportunity existed for slaves to become free businessmen, but for the most part, everyone knew their place. As long as everything prospered, people were fine with this system, and the occasional riot or strike was always quickly struck down.

Spiritually, the city was dead, with a wide variety of belief systems, each as errant as the one before it. While the official Roman Cult of the Emperor (that is, the emperor was worshiped as a deity) was hardly embraced by the populace, other beliefs thrived as people took to whatever new mystical, magical, or religious doctrine caught their fancy. This in turn led to inherent cynicism about new faiths, specifically Christianity. Most people of the time had a mix-and-match approach to their spirituality, borrowing whatever they liked from wherever they liked.

As for temples, there were dozens, all dedicated to different gods with Greek, Roman, Egyptian, Asian, and Persian names (some of them were even combinations; there was a temple to Zeus-Sarapis, for example). Each temple marketed itself well, with its own priests readily available to explain the god they worshiped and to accept sacrifices. Butcher shops were often connected with the temples to sell the meat after it was used in a ritual. But even in the midst of all this, the people were losing their attachment to the old gods. Sure, the gods were still supported by the state, and the temples were still financed as a means for wealthy men to show off their prosperity, but the people by and large didn't visit the temples on a daily basis. Instead, they lived for the many elaborate festivals, processions, and games the different cults used to get attention to their particular religion.

author: the apostle Paul

Paul started life in the small, prosperous city of Tarsus, and as he grew, he was educated in Greek rhetoric and literature and the Law of Moses as viewed by the Pharisees. Pharisaic teaching held that God had set Paul apart from other people in order to study the Law. Pharisees also believed that God would send a Messiah who looked very different from Jesus. Paul was one of the many Pharisees who opposed the thought of Jesus as Messiah, and was one of the first persecutors of early Christians.

Around AD 35, Jesus himself confronted Paul and revealed to him that he, Jesus, was indeed the Messiah and that Paul was only persecuting the God he loved (see Acts 9:1-19). Paul turned a new leaf and became devoted to Christ. Soon afterward, God sent him to the non-Jewish people of the world to proclaim the gospel, so he went on a tour of the known world, seeking out the Gentiles wherever they might be found. Eventually, this led him to the city of Ephesus.

plot: unity under any circumstance

Paul was a missionary for about seventeen years before he got to Ephesus, where, with the help of some fellow missionaries and some Christians already there, he founded a network of house churches. Most likely, his first converts were members of the existing Jewish population (the Jews were the fourth-largest group in Ephesus) and Gentiles who converted with some trepidation and without fully renouncing their old culture or undergoing circumcision. Most of these new Christians would have belonged to the middle class, and they were probably searching for truth and security, but not a total lifestyle and attitude change.

Interestingly, slaves and women were not allowed to choose their own religion, but if the head of their household became a Christian, everyone in that household did, including slaves and women. These were the people who formed the first Christian gatherings in Ephesus.

When Paul left Ephesus, he was focused on unifying these house-church networks into one organized body where all would agree on their mission and their collective place in the city. But he wound up getting imprisoned in Jerusalem instead. He was released, but he was arrested again and sent to Rome, where he wrote to Ephesus while imprisoned. Many scholars believe Paul intended this letter to make the rounds of his house-church network, not just in Ephesus, while others believe the letter was intended for non-Jewish Christians who'd converted after Paul left. Either way, the letter is written as though Paul had never met his readers.

Mystry - God's unfolding plan.

freedom!

In him we have redemption through his blood, the forgiveness of sins, in accordance with the riches of God's grace.

Ephesians 1:7

How many times have you been in a situation where something caused you to start talking to yourself? It probably wasn't because you consciously decided to converse with yourself; instead, you subconsciously knew that hearing yourself say things – *hearing* the actual words instead of just *thinking* them – was a much more potent way of getting the message across to yourself.

Similarly, house churches during Paul's time delivered readings aloud. A letter like Ephesians would've been spoken, or even intoned in a musical way, mainly because Greek vowels had a very musical sound to them. And instead of just sitting there and listening to the letter, everyone present – men and women, slaves and merchants – would have participated in the service, which usually consisted of someone singing or reading a line of text with the congregation members responding through repetition.

In this tradition, read Ephesians 1:1-14, first silently and then aloud.

1   You're going to be taking an in-depth look at the words of Paul, but before you do, read through the entire book of Ephesians in one sitting. Read it through as many times as you think it will take to get a general idea of what it's about. After you've read through the book, answer the following questions in preparation to dive in.

> **a** What's the overall tone of this letter? Why is Paul writing it?

> **b** In one brief sentence, state Paul's main message in Ephesians.

> **c** What repeated words do you keep seeing in Ephesians? Do they tie into any theme you detect?

> **d** What was Paul trying to accomplish with this letter?

e Check out the historical information on Ephesus in the introduction. Does it change your understanding or perception of the book of Ephesians? Why or why not?

fyi

• **Holy (1:4).** This word here means "set apart utterly for God," not just in words, but in character and actions that are given by God. In other words, holiness is a relationship to God.

• **Redemption (1:7).** A release from slavery or the death penalty, gained because someone paid the ransom.

• **When the times will have reached their fulfillment (1:10).** When Christ returns to the earth and establishes His kingdom here.

2 In 1:13, Paul says that Christians are "signed, sealed, and delivered" by the Holy Spirit (MSG). What does he mean by this?

3 Why did Paul start his letter with praise to God?

4   What do you hope to learn from the book of Ephesians as you journey through it? How do you want or expect your life to be affected?

5   Paul praises God for three different blessings in this passage. Choose one of them, then write three ways you could incorporate this praise into your own life. Meditate on it this week.

connect

Unless the members of your group already know each other well, this is a good opportunity to establish some trust and common ground, as well as learn where each person is coming from (and where you all want to go – both together and individually). Share a little bit about your histories; find out about each other. What are your first impressions of Ephesians? What are you each hoping to gain from your time together? Pray that you would develop closeness as a group as you journey through this study together.

go deeper

Paul shows his fondness of the word *free* in 1:1-14. Do a word study to find other places in the Bible where this word is used freely. Also, write about how Paul and other writers of Scripture associate freedom with Jesus' blood. How does Jesus' blood redeem us?

memory verse of the week

Did a particular verse make you think? Is there a verse you can't get out of your head? Write it down and memorize it. Allow God's Word to permanently brand itself in your head and your heart.

notes from group discussion

thanksgiving and prayer

I have not stopped giving thanks for you, remembering you in my prayers.

Ephesians 1:16

Has anything ever happened to you that left you speechless? Some act of kindness or generosity that caused you to bubble over with thankfulness? The credit card company inexplicably pardoning your late fees. The bread shop giving you a box of leftovers. Your boss telling you that, because it's such a nice day outside, you can knock off a little early. These are the unexpected niceties that make life pleasant.

That's the way Paul feels about the Ephesians. He's heard many great things about them, and so his heart is brewing a strong, ministerial connection toward them. He's positively filled with thankfulness for their support of him.

What do you do when you experience overwhelming thankfulness? In Paul's case, he prays.

Read Ephesians 1:15-23.

1 Connecting words give you clues about the ways different passages relate to each other. Verse 15 of Ephesians 1 starts with the words "For this reason." What does that tell you about the previous passage and the one to come?

fyi

• *Know him better (1:17).* This phrase means more than just a casual relationship. This is an intimate knowledge, the way a spouse knows his or her mate.

• *Heart (1:18).* The center of your thoughts, will, and emotions. The deepest part of your mind. The very soul of your being.

• *Hope (1:18).* This doesn't mean a mood or an emotional state; this is a tangible, real hope that comes from confidence in the promises of God.

2 What did Paul pray that the Ephesians would come to know more deeply about God?

3 Why is knowing Christ personally so important to achieving this?

4 Read 1:20-23. What is the relationship between Christ and the church? How does this relate to you?

Right hand (1:20). A king's right hand was a symbol of his power and authority.

5 How would you summarize this passage in your own words?

live

6 God's power raised Jesus from the dead, and is now in us (1:19-20). What does this mean for you?

7 Take some time to pray like Paul did in chapter 1 of Ephesians. Praise God, give thanks for specific things, then offer requests to Him for yourself and whomever else you might think of.

connect

In your group, share the most significant thing each of you learned about the hope, inheritance, and power you have as Christians. Discuss what day-to-day preoccupations keep you from focusing on these truths and how you can overcome them. Pray together for encouragement and boldness to live out what you've been learning.

go deeper

Paul talks a lot about physical, human things: strength, the head, feet, the body. Do some research about the physical body. How do our bodies become strong? What is the function and purpose of our heads? Our feet? Ask God to help you see how your natural body parallels the spiritual body known as the church.

memory verse of the week

Did a particular verse make you think? Is there a verse you can't get out of your head? Write it down and memorize it. Allow God's Word to permanently brand itself in your head and your heart.

notes from group discussion

stagnant no more

But because of his great love for us, God, who is rich in mercy, made us alive with Christ even when we were dead in transgressions – it is by grace you have been saved.

Ephesians 2:4-5

There's hardly anything more repulsive than water that's just been sitting around for days. Think of a child's wading pool, left in the sun. There the water is, roasting under heat and mild UV radiation, slowly becoming green with algae and other microorganisms, until it begins to stink. It's staining the sides of the pool now. It has rapidly deteriorated from being life-giving water to a substance that would readily make a person sick.

Paul paints a similar picture about a life of sin. It's a stagnant, deteriorating, infected life. But he promises us that through Christ, God refreshed us. He refilled our lives with pure, life-giving water. He renewed us. We have a new life, and only through Christ.

Read Ephesians 2:1-10.

1   Paul starts this chapter off by discussing how "you were dead in your transgressions and sins." In *The Message*, this reads "that old stagnant life of sin." Focus on this word *stagnant*. What does that mean? Write in your own words what it means to live a stagnant life, and contrast that with an active life.

2   Read 2:1-3 again. What was your life like before you found Christ's redemption? In what ways can you relate to this passage?

3   Read 2:4-10. According to verse 4, why did God save us from the consequences of our sin? How does verse 7 help us understand?

4   In your own words, list the things God has done for us, mentioned in 2:4-9.

5   Read 2:8-9. What is our part in responding to what God has done for us?

6 What's our purpose, according to verse 10?

fyi *Workmanship (2:10).* This suggests so much more than something that just rolled off the assembly line at the overseas factory. This is a handcrafted work of art, where the Creator invested himself in it.[1]

7 How does this passage relate to Ephesians 1?

live

8 Read Matthew 25:31-46 and 28:18-20. Is there anything you find in these two passages that relates to the "good work he has gotten ready for us to do" (MSG)?

9 What insights have you gained from this week's reading?

10 In *The Message*, 2:10 says that God created us by Christ Jesus to "join him in the work he does." Where would you place yourself on that journey?

connect

As a group, discuss the idea of being God's workmanship. What does it mean? How can you grow in your own awareness of this? How can you each individually live this out in a practical way? Pray together that this truth would be planted deeply in each of your hearts.

go deeper

Look up the words *grace* and *gracious* in a concordance or Bible study aid. Focus specifically on Paul's other letters. What else does he have to say about this topic?

memory verse of the week

Did a particular verse make you think? Is there a verse you can't get out of your head? Write it down and memorize it. Allow God's Word to permanently brand itself in your head and your heart.

Jews, meet the Gentiles

Lesson 4

But now in Christ Jesus you who once were far away have been brought near through the blood of Christ.

Ephesians 2:13

When it came to God, there used to be an invisible line that was drawn between the Jewish people and everyone else. As God's chosen people, the ones He'd given His laws to, the Jews were insiders; everyone else – those poor unfortunate people who didn't have the benefit of being born Jewish – was an outsider. The outsiders could not cross that line; the Jews were simply considered better. Think back to elementary school (or even high school, for that matter), where there was always that group of people on the playground (or in the lunch room) that stood out as exclusive and unapproachable and better.

With His sacrifice on the cross, Jesus erased that line. He put Jews and non-Jews (aka Gentiles) on equal ground. He made it okay to talk to that playground group. (Doesn't it seem absurd that we would obey such a line in the first place? But we do; we allow people to believe they are more valuable than we are.) Jesus had had enough of all this exclusivity, and He showed us that we are all on equal footing, because we are all children of God.

In the previous lesson, we saw that Paul explained what it means to become new both morally and spiritually as God's child. Now he moves on to talk about becoming new religiously and culturally. He teaches us about living without the wall.

Read Ephesians 2:11-22.

1   In 2:11-12, what does Paul say was a non-Jewish person's relationship to God?

Gentiles (2:11). This literally means "nations" or "ethnic groups," and is a term for non-Jews that has just an edge of contempt in it. The word *uncircumcised*, used later in the verse, was considered very contemptuous and derogatory.

fyi

2   What, according to verse 13, happened to change that relationship?

The law (2:15). This doesn't mean that Jesus did away with the eternal principles of God, but that He more specifically got rid of the old way that we humans tried to understand the law, as well as all the extra ceremony that came along with the Old Testament law. God hasn't changed; the way we approach Him, now through Christ, has.

fyi

3   How did Jesus repeal the law code and bring together Jews and Gentiles? What was the result of this?

4 Paul uses three different images in this lesson's passage as a vision of the ideal church. What are the images, and what do they teach us about our human relationships within the church?

2:15-16

2:19

2:20-22

fyi *Prophets (2:20).* This probably means not just Old Testament prophets, but also those in the early church with prophetic gifts (see Acts 11:27-28; 13:1).

5 How does this lesson's passage relate to the previous lesson's passage?

In the early goings of the church, Christianity was seen as a sect of Judaism, so many Jewish Christians began to feel superior to Gentile Christians. Paul had to write a harsh rebuke to these Jews in order to set the record straight. A decade later, the tables had turned, and Gentiles, who knew only Paul's harsh words, began to question the legitimacy of Jewish Christians. Paul reminded them, in the form of the book of Ephesians, that no one is holier than anyone else.

6 Now that you've studied it, summarize this week's passage in your own words.

live

7 Read over your responses to the questions above. Pray and ask the Lord to reveal to you one thing that you can change about the way you relate to other people. Then record specific, practical steps that can help you in your quest.

connect

Discuss with your group the images Paul uses to make the point about Christ making us one. Does anyone have any questions? As a group, try to think of a few ways you can tear down the walls within the church and create the ideal church that Paul speaks of. Pray that God will give you wisdom and strength as you implement these suggestions this week.

go deeper

In 2:12, Paul talks about "God's covenants and promises in Israel" (MSG). Use a Bible study aid to determine what some of those covenants and promises were.

memory verse of the week

Did a particular verse make you think? Is there a verse you can't get out of your head? Write it down and memorize it. Allow God's Word to brand itself permanently in your head and your heart.

notes from group discussion

God's secret plan

Lesson 5

Surely you have heard about the administration of God's grace that was given to me for you, that is, the mystery made known to me by revelation.

Ephesians 3:2-3

Has anyone ever thrown you a surprise party? Perhaps you were simply expecting to have dinner with a few people, and when you arrived at their home, SURPRISE! – the living room is full of friends and family. You begin to realize that all the clues were there; if you'd been looking for them, you'd have figured out the surprise. But you're glad you didn't.

God had a secret plan too, a plan that would unite Jews and non-Jews and create a new church. But no one knew about it until Christ came, and then the surprise was let out of the bag. If the people of the time had been looking for the clues, they'd have seen them.

Read Ephesians 3:1-13.

1   Read 3:1-2 and 7-8. What was Paul's attitude toward his ministry?

2   What does that attitude teach us about the way we should serve God?

> ***Mystery (3:3).*** Ephesus was flooded with mysterious, secret **fyi**
> cults that required expensive, bizarre initiation ceremonies.
> At the same time, a way of thinking called Gnosticism was also being
> developed, which held that the world was a disastrous place that
> needed to be ignored. However, Gnostics considered their philosophy
> a "mystery" that was only for the select few to know. When Paul used
> the word ***mystery*** in this verse, he was pointing out the lunacy of the
> mystery cults and Gnosticism. God kept his secret until it was time to
> reveal it, and now that the cat was out of the bag, it was time to let
> everyone know.

3   Read 3:9-10. What was God's timetable for bringing about his plan?

4   Explain God's purpose in this plan.

48

• **_Freedom (3:12)._** The word in this context denotes a legal right to speak freely and fearlessly in front of a ruler or king.[1]

• **_Discouraged (3:13)._** To lose strength by becoming lazy, tired, desperate, and despondent.[2]

• **_Glory (3:13)._** Honor that comes from people having a good opinion of you.[3] If this word is used when talking about God, it also means a spiritual radiance that reflects God's worthiness to be praised.

5 Describe Paul's attitude toward the suffering he's living through because of Christ.

6 What is the main message of this passage?

live

7 Read 3:8. Do you ever feel this way about God? Think of a few practical ways that God has equipped you to deliver his message.

8 How can you acquire Paul's attitude toward suffering (mentioned in verse 13)?

connect

Paul's mission was to spill the beans about God's salvation for both Jews and Gentiles. In your group, share your individual responses about your own personal mission. What is it? How does it tie into Paul's, if at all? How can you know your mission? How prepared are you to face the type of suffering in carrying out your mission that Paul did in carrying out his? Share with each other the ways you've been progressing through this study, and encourage each other to keep on seeking personal progress. Pray for wisdom as each of you carries out your part of God's secret plan.

go deeper

In verse 13, Paul mentions his "present trouble" (MSG). Read 1 Corinthians 4:9-13 and 2 Corinthians 11:24-29 to discover what he's talking about. Summarize it here, in your own words.

memory verse of the week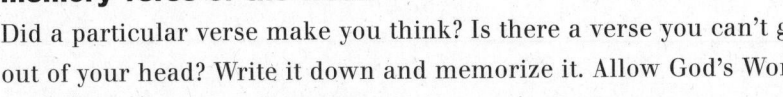

Did a particular verse make you think? Is there a verse you can't get out of your head? Write it down and memorize it. Allow God's Word to permanently brand itself in your head and your heart.

God can do anything

Lesson 6

Now to him who is able to do immeasurably more than all we ask or imagine, according to his power that is at work within us, to him be glory in the church and in Christ Jesus throughout all generations, for ever and ever! Amen.

Ephesians 3:20-21

What if there were some sort of medicine you could take that would boost your confidence in any way you wanted? Afraid of public speaking? Take this, and suddenly you're the most gifted orator in the world. Want to be a fighter pilot, but you're afraid of heights? One drop and you're SuperFlyer.

While it isn't a miracle drug, Christ's love does open up a realm of confidence we'd never know without it. His Spirit works within us to bring about change in our hearts, and an unrelenting faith in God's ability to do anything. With Christ in us, we can have greater confidence than any human concoction could offer.

Read Ephesians 3:14-21.

1 Paul has reminded the people about their former condition and how God is transforming them. He's also reminded them of his own mission. Now, in this week's lesson, Paul is praying for the Ephesians. How did the truths of chapter 2 lead to this prayer?

2 Read 3:14-15. What does this passage tell you about Paul's attitude toward God? Toward God's sovereignty?

• *Family (3:15)*. Human families, angelic families, and the local church—these all fit under the word *family* that is used here.

• *Name (3:15)*. Jews believed that names went beyond their meanings; if you gave something a name, you held authority over it.

• *Inner being (3:16)*. Paul is addressing many people who were recent converts, and while their spirits—their inner beings—had been made alive, they were still weak or asleep, much like a newborn baby needs strength. (See also Romans 7:22; 1 Corinthians 3:1-3; 2 Corinthians 4:16; Ephesians 5:14.)

3   Read Paul's prayer in 3:16-19. Describe what you believe to be his primary emphasis in this prayer.

4   Read 3:20-21. What does this tell you about God? About your relationship with Him? About His purpose for all believers?

5   What truth in this passage about God's love means the most to you? Why?

live

6   Go back to 3:16-19. How can you relate to the prayers Paul claimed for the Ephesians? Rewrite a part of the prayer that affected you most, and insert words that describe your current life to make this prayer specifically about you.

7   Write Paul's prayer in 3:16-19 on a note card or piece of paper. Hang it in a place that you see daily, and use it as a prayer guide for yourself and others.

connect

As a group, spend some time in serious prayer for each other, much in the same way Paul prayed for the Ephesians. Share your requests, then lift each other up in prayer. Also, pray for the strengthening of the church as a whole. You can also discuss ways to help one another use the gifts of power and love.

go deeper

Try writing an outline of 3:14-21 in order to get the full picture of what Paul is saying. How does this passage relate to Ephesians 1 and 2? Write down your thoughts.

memory verse of the week

Did a particular verse make you think? Is there a verse you can't get out of your head? Write it down and memorize it. Allow God's Word to permanently brand itself in your head and your heart.

notes from group discussion

time to grow up

Then we will no longer be infants, tossed back and forth by the waves, and blown here and there by every wind of teaching and by the cunning and craftiness of men in their deceitful scheming. Instead, speaking the truth in love, we will in all things grow up into him who is the Head, that is, Christ.

Ephesians 4:14-15

There comes a time when it's no longer acceptable to color outside the lines. Or to read books that solely involve learning to count or seeing Spot run. And there comes a time when eating paste or crayons becomes foolish instead of cute. Eventually, we need to grow up and move on to the next stage of maturity.

Paul encourages the Ephesian Christians in this manner because he sees their tendency to not want to grow up. He challenges them to start interacting with their world and wrestling with the high and difficult truths of the Christian faith. He wants them to grow up so they can travel the road God wants them to travel.

Read Ephesians 4:1-16.

1 Paul uses the word *then* in 4:1, connecting chapters 1–3 to what is about to follow. What does this phrase lead you to expect in chapters 4–6?

> *Calling (4:1).* This word *calling* suggests more than a purpose; it suggests that the calling itself is for those of high and honorable status.
>
> fyi

2 Read 4:2-3. In verse 2, Paul lists three character traits we should possess. What are they? How do they prepare us for the command he gives in verse 3?

> *Humble . . . gentle . . . patient (4:2).* To the non-Christian of the time, these three things would be highly undesirable in anyone of status. Humility, or the willingness to take little honor or to give higher place to someone else, was the way a slave or someone with no self-respect would act. Gentleness, or meekness, was foreign to the Greeks, who definitely had a "might makes right" view of the world. And patience, or self-restraint in the face of provocation,[1] was just downright unnecessary.
>
> fyi

3 Read 4:4-6. What is Paul's central, unifying declaration? How does this shed light on the first three chapters of Ephesians?

fyi *Descended (4:9).* Some scholars believe Paul meant that Christ descended into what's known as Abraham's Bosom (where Old Testament God-followers went after they died, as they had not yet had an opportunity to accept Christ's sacrifice as the way into heaven) to preach the gospel to everyone there. Others believe Paul is referring to Christ descending to the lowest state of the universe—death.[2]

4 Read 4:11-13. What else has Christ given us? Why?

fyi *Mature (4:13).* This literally means "a mature man." The original Greek suggests that not only are believers in Christ meant to be mature individuals, but also that God intends to form all believers together into one new man—Christ.

5 According to 4:13-15, what are the chief signs of spiritual maturity and immaturity?

6 What does it mean to "know the whole truth and tell it in love," as stated in 4:15 (MSG)? What is an example of telling the truth *not* in love?

7　Read 4:13. In what is our unity based? Write three practical implications this verse has for your own life.

8　Read 4:15-16. What does this metaphor for the church tell you about your own spiritual growth?

connect

Paul urges us to know the truth and tell it in love. Discuss this idea in your group, with each of you sharing ways you have done this. Have you ever known the truth but *not* told it in love? What happened? How does this disrupt the type of unity Paul is encouraging us to strive for? Discuss some ways you can start achieving unity in your own group, and pray for this kind of togetherness and love to work through each member of your group.

go deeper

Read 4:2. Any of those words (*humble, gentle, patient*) would make a good word study. Grab a few Bible study aids and see what's written about these topics in the rest of the New Testament, or read through the Gospels and see what Jesus had to say about them.

memory verse of the week

Did a particular verse make you think? Is there a verse you can't get out of your head? Write it down and memorize it. Allow God's Word to permanently brand itself in your head and your heart.

the old way has to go

You were taught, with regard to your former way of life, to put off your old self, which is being corrupted by its deceitful desires; to be made new in the attitude of your minds; and to put on the new self, created to be like God in true righteousness and holiness.

Ephesians 4:22-24

Some people will cling to the VCR as long as they can, instead of making the switch to DVD. Others insist that no good music has been made since 1972, when rock and roll achieved perfection. And in some minds, iPods will never be better than Walkmans, laptops will never be superior to typewriters, and antennae will never ever be superceded by something like digital cable.

These people are entitled to their opinions, but there are certain times when we need to accept innovation and let the old way go. Like when we accept Christ; that is the time to realize that a life of sin is inferior to life with Christ, so the things we did and clung to in our life of sin need to go in the trash with the rabbit-ear antenna.

Read Ephesians 4:17-32.

1 Read 4:17-19. How does Paul describe the lives of the ungodly?

Sensuality (4:19). More than likely, this has to do with ritual prostitution and other practices at the pagan temples of Ephesus.

fyi

2 Why does Paul "insist" that Christians not go along with the crowd?

3 Are there any warnings here for Christians? What are they?

4 What are the three things Paul mentions in 4:22-24 about the way God changes our lives? Do you think Paul intends these as three consecutive steps? Why or why not?

Corrupted (4:22). Think of something rotting, decaying, dying, or dead. That's what this word means here.[1]

5   Check out what Jesus says in Matthew 12:33-37. How does this help us understand why Paul commanded 4:22-24 *before* he commanded 4:25-32?

6   Are 4:25 and 4:29 somehow connected to each other? If so, how?

7   In 4:32, how does Paul recommend we forgive each other? Why is this important to our relationships with others?

8   How does this passage of teaching relate to 4:1-16?

live

9   Read 4:20-24, where Paul summarizes the things the Ephesians had learned about Christ. How can you put these things into practice? Write down some concrete ways.

10 Think of some practical ways to obey the command in 4:26-27.

11 List the character traits Paul mentions in 4:32. How can you practically demonstrate these in your own life?

connect

Discuss 4:22-24. Read it aloud, then talk about how to put it into practice, each member sharing a way to apply it to himself or herself. In Galatians 6:2, we are urged to share one another's burdens. With this in mind, read through 4:25-32. Individually share which trait is a personal struggle. As a group, encourage each other and look for practical ways to help each other through these struggles. Pray for strength and encouragement, and make a plan to check up on each other once or twice before your group meets again.

go deeper

Look up Romans 8:5-6 and 12:1-2. What do you find there that potentially sheds light on 4:22-24? Write down everything you see.

memory verse of the week

Did a particular verse make you think? Is there a verse you can't get out of your head? Write it down and memorize it. Allow God's Word to permanently brand itself in your head and your heart.

wake up!

Lesson 9

Be very careful, then, how you live – not as unwise but as wise, making the most of every opportunity, because the days are evil.

Ephesians 5:15-16

It happens all the time, especially if you aren't a morning person. The alarm goes off; you hit the snooze. Repeat two or three or eight times before you finally drag yourself out of bed. If you're lucky, you won't mismatch your socks or do anything else boneheaded until you've fully shaken off your night's sleep and are, in fact, awake.

It's too bad that there's no snooze button on life. Especially in a life guided by Christ. We are not allowed to sleepwalk through this existence; instead, we are called to be vigilant and intelligent in the way we live.

Paul made it clear in chapters 1–3 that salvation is an unearned gift from God. Then in chapter 4 he gave us a reason to live ethically in light of that gift. Now he offers ways to put those previous concepts into practice.

Read Ephesians 5:1-20.

1a What are some of the reasons Paul has already given for ethical living?

1b What reasons does he add in these verses?

    5:2

    5:5-6

    5:8

    5:11

    5:15-16

2　What purposes and goals in life would you need to have in order to live the "life of love" Paul commands in 5:1-2?

3　Read 5:3-4. What are some of the things Paul is warning Christians against? What kinds of thoughts or actions should we be vigilant in guarding?

fyi　*Immorality (5:3).* This comes from the Greek word *porneia* (the root of the English word *pornography*), and it means illicit sexual activity.

4　Read 5:6-7. In verse 7, why does Paul say not to "hang around" the people he describes in verse 6 (msg)?

5　Read 5:8-14. What are the characteristics of light? Of darkness?

fyi　• *Find out (5:10).* This doesn't mean to find out by hearsay or rumor, but actually by experience.

• *Expose (5:11).* Paul is encouraging the Ephesians to do more than just *say* that the deeds of darkness are fruitless; his instruction is to *prove* that fruitlessness by living a fruitful life — a life in line with the Word of God.

• *Foolish (5:17).* The word Paul used here included shades of hard-headedness, panic, and compulsive behavior.

6   Read 5:19-20. What does this passage show us about our relationship with God?

live

7   What are some practical ways you can live a "life of love"?

8   Are you struggling with any of the hang-ups mentioned in this passage? What does Paul say about dealing with those unholy habits? How can you put his advice into practice in your own life? Pray about this area, and seek wise counsel from mature Christians if necessary.

connect

If you're comfortable, share with the group an area of your life that needs to be exposed to the light of Christ. Encourage each other, and pray together for strength to invite God into that area. Thank God for His wonderful light and for the transformation it brings. (Note: This is an opportunity for some real healing to happen within your group; however, since this exercise can often delve into the topic of sexual addiction, it may be especially sensitive in mixed-gender groups.)

go deeper

Study the image of "light" as it is used elsewhere in the New Testament. Start with Paul's other letters, Jesus' words, and the book of 1 John.

memory verse of the week

Did a particular verse make you think? Is there a verse you can't get out of your head? Write it down and memorize it. Allow God's Word to permanently brand itself in your head and your heart.

husbands, wives

"**For** this reason a man will leave his father and mother and be united to his wife, and the two will become one flesh." This is a profound mystery – but I am talking about Christ and the church.

Ephesians 5:31-32

Most of us have endured the boss who we just absolutely couldn't stand. The one who was on a power trip and who seemed to get a kick out of making life as miserable as possible. Life within the Roman Empire could be like that if you weren't a man, because men were the undisputed master of their wives, children, and slaves, no matter how they treated them..

Into this mentality came Paul's letter to the Ephesians as a reminder that, whether you were the master or the servant, you needed to maintain the perspective of the *real* relationship at work: the one between Christ and his church. There was a fear in that time that the Christian way of life would destroy the societal norm, but Paul claimed that instead of changing society, Christ wanted to change individual hearts (although, in that case, society would inevitably change).

Read Ephesians 5:21-33.

• *Reverence (5:21).* This literally means "fear," like trembling in the holy presence of God, knowing full well His capacity for judging you.

fyi

• *Submit (5:21-22).* Voluntary demotion. This term was usually reserved for the military, where it was used as a way to get the point across to lower ranks that they were to submit to the higher ranks. Neither Greeks nor Jews associated it with marriage.

1   Read 5:21. What's the general attitude that Christians should have toward one another? What are some words and phrases that define this attitude for you?

2   What motive does Paul give for his command in verse 21? What are the practical implications of this for those in authority? For those under authority?

3   Paul offers advice to both husbands and wives in regard to making their marriages work. What instructions does he give wives? Husbands?

4   Read 5:23-24, where Paul uses the husband/wife relationship as an analogy with the Christ/church relationship. In the context of this analogy, what does "leadership" mean? What about a wife's support of her husband? A husband's love for his wife?

5   Read 5:33. What are the attitudes a husband and wife should have toward each other?

6   In 5:21-33, what are the most important keys for a wife to use toward understanding her role in the marriage? What about a husband?

live

7   What insights have you gained from 5:21-33? Have you changed your behavior because of this passage? Do you plan to? Write down a few specific ways you plan to make this happen.

connect

Whether the people in your group are married or single, talk about the principles of submission to one another and the parallels between marriage and Christ and His church. Does anyone have any questions? Try to answer them, or at least search for the answers as a group, underscoring your answers with Scripture. Questions about marital relations can be difficult; take the extra time necessary to seek out substantive answers. Pray together for the strength and ability to submit to one another.

go deeper

Look up other words along the lines of this topic (*respect, honor, submit, serve, love,* and so on) to see what else the Bible has to say. Be sure to pay attention to the context of the verses you find.

Compare this passage to Genesis 2:18-24. What sort of relationship did God intend husbands and wives to have? How do these two passages fit together?

memory verse of the week

Did a particular verse make you think? Is there a verse you can't get out of your head? Write it down and memorize it. Allow God's Word to permanently brand itself in your head and your heart.

notes from group discussion

children, parents, servants, masters

Lesson 11

Serve wholeheartedly, as if you were serving the Lord, not men.

Ephesians 6:7

Who knows everything there is to know about relationships? Anyone? Is anyone raising a hand out there? Truth is, we all have something to learn about relationships, and not just the husband/wife kind of relationship either. We're basically clueless when it comes to relating best with our parents, our bosses, our employees, our fellow human beings. None of us has the perfect answer.

Paul understood that one of the key aspects of a relationship is that it flows both ways. Both people in a relationship receive and both people give, even in the case when one person is an authority figure and the other person isn't. Paul has something to say about this give-and-take, this back-and-forth relationship flow, and no one is exempt from his commands.

Read Ephesians 6:1-9.

1   Why does Paul tell children that obedience "is only right" (MSG)?

2   What does it mean to "honor" one's parents?

3   Read 6:1-3. What is the promise Paul quotes along with the commandment? Why did God link this promise with this commandment?

4   In verse 4, Paul tells fathers not to exasperate their children. What do you think it looks like when a parent does that? Do you ever experience this with your parents? Write down any ways you feel your parents have exasperated you. Then write specifically how you think Paul would suggest you handle it.

5 In contrast, what are some practical ways a father might "bring [his children] up in the training and instruction of the Lord"?

6 Read 6:5-9. How do verses 6 and 7 explain the instruction given in verse 5?

7 What kinds of attitudes was Paul trying to teach servants in verse 8? What attitudes was he trying to keep them from? How can we incorporate these positive attitudes in our modern culture?

8 In verse 9, what does Paul mean when he says "in the same way"?

9 What sort of attitudes should a master have? What should he avoid?

10 What is the central teaching of this week's passage from Ephesians?

11 What are your attitudes toward your own parents? To discern your honest feelings, pray about them. Are they feelings of honor or dishonor? How should you handle these feelings?

12 If you have a job, think about it in the context of 6:5-9. Write a few practical ways to incorporate into your daily work the attitudes Paul encourages. What would be the easiest to put into practice? The most difficult? Pray about these.

Take some time as a group to discuss parent-child relationships, as well as ethics in the workplace. Share a time when you were able to put Paul's words into practice, whether it was with your parents, or with a boss or teacher. Do you remember an instance when you *didn't* put these words into practice? What happened? Pray as a group, asking God to give you a proper perspective on submission.

go deeper

Write an outline of 5:21–6:9. What are the main points Paul is trying to get across? What does the rest of the Bible have to say about these points?

memory verse of the week

Did a particular verse make you think? Is there a verse you can't get out of your head? Write it down and memorize it. Allow God's Word to permanently brand itself in your head and your heart.

notes from group discussion

a fight to the finish

Lesson 12

For our struggle is not against flesh and blood, but against the rulers, against the authorities, against the powers of this dark world and against the spiritual forces of evil in the heavenly realms.

Ephesians 6:12

So, we've learned a lot about who we are in Christ, and the way we ought to live, and how we should treat each other. But why did we need to learn these things? Because they are preparation. Preparation for a battle.

Many times, we learn things not knowing that we'll need them later; they get buried a little bit, underneath the surfaces of our hearts. But when we get in the midst of a sticky situation, something we think we aren't equipped to handle, we discover that if we dig a little deeper, we'll find those preparatory tools right where we need them.

Truth be known, we are in a fight. We have an enemy, and we have been prepared to square off with him. No matter how kind or passive we are, we are in a battle, and the stakes are high.

Read Ephesians 6:10-24.

1   What does it mean to you that God wants you strong, as implied in 6:10?

Can (6:11). This could be translated literally as "will have power to." Insert this phrase for the word *can* in 6:11 and read the verse aloud.

fyi

2   In 6:12, Paul says our fight against the Devil and all his angels is "no afternoon athletic contest" (MSG). What sort of fight is it? What is the end goal?

3   How can we prepare for this fight?

• **Stand your ground (6:13).** In the original Greek, Paul used this word as a military term that meant something like "holding a critical position in a battlefield."[1]

fyi

• **Truth . . . righteousness . . . salvation (6:14-17).** God promised these gifts in his covenant, and they are signs of his kingdom. See Isaiah 59:15-21.

• **Readiness (6:15).** Along the lines of "steadfastness,"[2] like you're wearing very firm boots.

4   How are truth, righteousness, peace, faith, and salvation weapons in our fight against the Devil?

5   Paul mentions God's Word (probably not just the Old Testament but also the preaching of the gospel and prayer) as being "an indispensable weapon" in 6:17 (MSG). How can it be used both offensively and defensively?

6   In what ways can prayer be both a preparation for battle and the battle itself?

7 Read 6:18-20. What are the different instructions Paul gives on how to pray? Write down all you find and your own personal measurement on how well you practice them.

8 Read 6:21-24. What can you learn from this passage about relationships between Christians in the early church?

9 Reread the entire book of Ephesians. What have you learned about who you are in Christ? God's goal for the church? Your mission? The way you should live? Prayer?

live

10 Meditate on the weapons of God that Paul mentions in 6:14-17. What are some practical ways you can put them to use in your life? Pray for the wisdom to use them when necessary.

11 What does Paul's prayer request in 6:19-20 suggest about your own intercession for people who are spreading the gospel? And for your presentation of the gospel to those who've never heard it?

12 Think back on some of the choices you've made to change your lifestyle according to what you've learned in this study. Are you content with your follow-through? Has anything new come to mind that you'd like to change? Pray about these things.

connect

Paul was writing to whole congregations, not just individuals. As a group, discuss the armor of God and the meaning and significance of each piece. We are not meant to fight our battles alone, so spend some time together as a group, praying for each other. Pray for wisdom in the battle and that God would strengthen each of you as you fight against your common enemy. Wrap up your time by reflecting on what you've each learned in your time together, and discuss the changes you've seen in each other and in yourselves.

Head to the library or bookstore and do some research on armor, especially the kind the ancient Romans used. Paul wrote Ephesians while in prison, so he saw lots of armed guards. What did this armor look like? What purpose did it serve? What does it mean for you to "put on" this armor? Apply to your life all that you learn through your research.

memory verse of the week

Did a particular verse make you think? Is there a verse you can't get out of your head? Write it down and memorize it. Allow God's Word to permanently brand itself in your head and your heart.

notes from group discussion

study resources

It's true that studying the Bible can often lead you to answers for life's tough questions. But Bible study also prompts plenty of *new* questions. Perhaps you're intrigued by a passage and want to understand it better. Maybe you're stumped about what a particular verse or word means. Where do you go from here? Study resources can help. Research a verse's history, cultural context, and connotations. Look up unfamiliar words. Track down related Scripture passages elsewhere in the Bible. Study resources can help sharpen your knowledge of God's Word.

Below you'll find a selected bibliography of study resources. Use them to discover more, dig deeper, and ultimately grow closer to God.

a study resource collection

TH1NK REFERENCE COLLECTION: *The Bible: Think for Yourself About What's Inside; Theology: Think for Yourself About What You Believe; Worldviews: Think for Yourself About How We See God.* Colorado Springs, CO: NavPress, 2006.

historical and background sources

Carson, D. A., Douglas Moo, and Leon Morris. *An Introduction to the New Testament.* Grand Rapids, MI: Zondervan, 1992.

Provides an overview of the New Testament for students and teachers. Covers historical and biographical information and includes outlines and discussions of each book's theological importance.

Packer, James I., Merrill C. Tenney, and William White Jr. *The Bible Almanac*. Nashville: Nelson, 1980.

> *Contains information about people of the Bible and how they lived. Photos and illustrations help the characters come to life.*

Tenney, Merrill C. *New Testament Survey*. Grand Rapids, MI: Eerdmans, 1985.

> *Analyzes social, political, cultural, economic, and religious backgrounds of each New Testament book.*

concordances, dictionaries, and atlases

concordances

If you are studying a specific word and want to know where to find it in the Bible, use a concordance. A concordance lists every verse in the Bible in which that word shows up. An *exhaustive* concordance includes every word in a given translation (there are different concordances for different Bible translations), and an *abridged* or *complete* concordance leaves out some words, some occurrences of the words, or both. Multiple varieties exist, so choose for yourself which one you like best. *Strong's Exhaustive Concordance* and *Young's Analytical Concordance of the Bible* are the most popular.

bible dictionaries

Sometimes called a Bible encyclopedia, a Bible dictionary alphabetically lists articles about people, places, doctrines, important words, customs, and geography of the Bible. Here are a few to consider:

The New Strong's Expanded Dictionary of Bible Words. Nashville: Nelson, 2001.

> *Defines more than 14,000 words. In addition, it includes an index that gives meanings of the word in the original language.*

Nelson's New Illustrated Bible Dictionary. Nashville: Nelson, 1996.
> *Includes over 500 photos, maps, and pronunciation guides.*

The New Unger's Bible Dictionary. Wheaton, IL: Moody, 1988.
> *Displays pictures, maps, and illustrations. Clearly written, easy to understand, and compatible with most Bible translations.*

Vine's Expository Dictionary of New Testament Words. Peabody, MA: Hendrickson, 1993.
> *Lists major words and defines each New Testament Greek word.*

bible atlases

We often skim over mentions of specific locations in the Bible, but location is an important element to understanding the context of a passage. A Bible atlas can help you understand the geography in a book of the Bible and how it may have affected the recorded events. Here are two good choices:

The Illustrated Bible Atlas. Grand Rapids, MI: Kregel, 1999.
> *Provides concise (and colorful) information on lands and cities where events took place. Includes historical notes.*

The Carta Bible Atlas. Jerusalem: Carta, 2003.
> *Includes analytical notes on biblical events, military campaigns, travel routes, and archeological highlights, as well as indexes. A very popular atlas for students, scholars, and clergy.*

for small-group leaders

If you are the leader of a small group or would like to lead a small group, these resources may help:

Beyerlein, Ann. *Small Group Leaders' Handbook*. Downers Grove, IL: InterVarsity, 1995.

> *Teaches the biblical basis and growth stages of small groups. Helps leaders develop skills for resolving conflict, leading discussion, and planning for the future.*

McBride, Neal F. *How to Lead Small Groups*. Colorado Springs, CO: NavPress, 1990.

> *Covers leadership skills for all kinds of small groups. Filled with step-by-step guidance and practical exercises focusing on the most important aspects of small-group leadership.*

Polich, Laurie. *Help! I'm a Small-Group Leader*. Grand Rapids, MI: Zondervan, 1998.

> *Offers tips and solutions to help you nurture your small group and accomplish your goals. Suggests techniques and questions to use in many Bible study circumstances.*

bible study methods

Fee, Gordon, and Douglas Stuart. *How to Read the Bible for All Its Worth*. Grand Rapids, MI: Zondervan, 2003.

> *Offers chapters on interpreting and applying the different kinds of writing in the Bible: the Epistles, the Gospels, Old Testament Law, Old Testament narrative, the Prophets, Psalms, Wisdom Literature, and Revelation. Also includes suggestions for commentaries on each book of the Bible.*

LaHaye, Tim. *How to Study the Bible for Yourself*. Eugene, OR: Harvest House, 1998.

> *Teaches how to illuminate Scripture through study. Gives methods for understanding the Bible's major principles, promises, commands, key verses, and themes.*

Wald, Oletta. *The New Joy of Discovery in Bible Study.* Minneapolis: Augsburg, 2002.

Helps students of Scripture discover how to observe all that is in a text, how to ask questions of a text, and how to use grammar and passage structure to see the writer's point. Teaches methods for independent Bible study.

notes

Lesson 3: Stagnant No More
1. Markus Barth, *Ephesians 1–3, Anchor Study Bible*, vol. 34 (Garden City, NY: Doubleday, 1974), 226.

Lesson 5: God's Secret Plan
1. Markus Barth, *Ephesians 1–3, Anchor Study Bible*, vol. 34 (Garden City, NY: Doubleday, 1974), 330.
2. Barth, 349.
3. "Glory" in W. E. Vine, *An Expository Dictionary of New Testament Words* (Nashville: Royal Publishers, 1952), 483.

Lesson 7: Time to Grow Up
1. W. E. Vine, *An Expository Dictionary of New Testament Words* (Nashville: Royal Publishers, 1952), 840.
2. Francis Foulkes, *The Epistle of Paul to the Ephesians, Tyndale New Testament Commentaries* (Grand Rapids, MI: Eerdmans, 1981), 116.

Lesson 8: The Old Way Has to Go
1. Markus Barth, *Ephesians 4–6, Anchor Study Bible*, vol. 34 (Garden City, NY: Doubleday, 1974), 502.

Lesson 10: Husbands, Wives
1. Markus Barth, *Ephesians 4–6, Anchor Study Bible*, vol. 34 (Garden City, NY: Doubleday, 1974), 631.

Lesson 12: A Fight to the Finish
1. Markus Barth, *Ephesians 4–6, Anchor Study Bible*, vol. 34 (Garden City, NY: Doubleday, 1974), 762.
2. Barth, 770.

More TH1NK Double-Edged Bible Studies from NavPress.

TH1NK: LIFECHANGE Mark
The Navigators
978-1-57683-692-7
This close look at the first of the written Gospels will help you encounter God in a new way.

TH1NK: LIFECHANGE James
The Navigators
978-1-57683-691-0
This in-depth study of James will empower you to grow spiritually and go deeper into God's Word.

TH1NK: LIFECHANGE Ruth & Esther
The Navigators
978-1-57683-852-5
Young women will find two strong examples of women who lived for God, no matter what the cost.

TH1NK: LIFECHANGE Romans
The Navigators
978-1-57683-850-1
With this fresh study of Romans, you'll learn to identify, study, and apply foundational theological concepts.

TH1NK: LIFECHANGE John
The Navigators
978-1-60006-001-4
John 3:16 only scratches the surface of this important book. Get into this one-of-a-kind gospel with an in-depth study of John.

To order copies, call NavPress at 1-800-366-7788 or
log on to www.navpress.com.

NAVPRESS
Discipleship Inside Out™